CIVIC PRIDE

Sculpture has helped to express the identity of towns and cities for centuries. *The Black Prince (1)* in City Square has become a potent symbol of Leeds and monumental centrepiece of this urban public space, though few know why he's there. The first monarch to be commemorated in Leeds was *Queen Anne (16)* in 1712, but the heyday for commemorative statues was the nineteenth century when Leeds aspired to become a northern centre for the arts. Statues of national heroes and local men, whose works had helped define the character of the emerging town, were often erected by public subscription and encouraged a sense of civic pride.

For the founders of Leeds Art Gallery, and Alderman W Harding in particular, public sculpture was another means of encouraging interest in the fine arts whilst making the city a more pleasant place to be. Doubtless the noted twentieth-century sculptor, Henry Moore (educated at Leeds Art College), recognised this as he left his own legacy in the form of The Henry Moore Institute and Centre for the Study of Sculpture. One of Moore's works is on loan to the city from the *Henry Moore Foundation (15)*. Latterly, public sculpture has commemorated the twinning of Leeds with Dortmund in Germany with a symbol of the Altien Brewery, the *Dortmund Drayman (34)*. Leeds businesses have also enlivened the commercial centre with works by young sculptors and established practitioners. The University of Leeds is a continuing patron and courageously went ahead with the city's most controversial piece, the *Eric Gill (28)* Not all controversial pieces fare so well, however as in the recent case of Anthony Gormley's Brick Man which failed to find a home in Leeds.

The works of several celebrated sculptors can be found in the city. The first English sculptor to gain an international reputation was John Flaxman, whose monument to Captains Walker and Beckett is to be found in the Parish Church (see appendix). This was soon followed by the work of one of the country's most noted portrait sculptors, *Francis Chantrey (20)*. William Behnes was arguably one of the most able portraitists of the Victorian period, and was responsible for Leeds's icon of Victorian politics, *Sir Robert Peel (25)*, whilst the ubiquitous *Victoria Memorial (26)* was the work of a distinguished practitioner of the New Sculpture movement, Sir George Frampton. Active around the end of the nineteenth century, the New Sculptors aimed to bring a fresh vitality to sculpture, through colour and movement as well as in variety of materials. Bronze was favoured over white marble for its expressive qualities. Leeds has an impressive collection of their work in City Square. The twentieth century saw a further reaction again, a demand for truth to materials and direct, hands-on carving. In the two war memorials by HC Fehr and Eric Gill the contrast between old and new can clearly be seen *(17 and 28)*. The City Art Galleries contain several fine pieces of sculpture, but they are outside the scope of this guide.

The unveiling of City Square statuary 1903

Leeds's impressive collection of public sculpture has nevertheless been subject to the vagaries of changing taste and the perils of the motor car, several statues have themselves gone 'walkabout'. Many are now recognised as the works of sculptors outstanding among European artists of their time and the city's aspiring role as an international centre of sculpture augurs well for the return of works to their original settings. The *Queen Victoria Memorial (26)* once stood outside the Town Hall, flanked by *Sir Robert Peel (25)* and the *Duke of Wellington (24)*. City Square's sculptural scheme, once rivalling those of major European cities in providing both an impressive gateway and grand civic centrepiece, is now severely reduced with its balustrades removed, several bronze lights missing and Drury's nymphs in an ignominious line. The remaining works of art need careful repositioning if they are again to symbolise corporate life.

Some of the most successful cities in Europe and America still define urban spaces with newly-commissioned civic sculptures by leading sculptors bringing interest, colour and amusement as well as providing necessary respite from the bustle of city life. In Leeds the Civic Trust and the City Council aim to restore City Square's former glory. Both the Civic Trust and the City Council are committed to a policy of conservation and new development and to making Leeds once more a city centre for the arts.

The trail is divided into two separate tours. Anyone wishing to complete the trail in one journey should leave Tour One after the War Memorial (17) and walk to the Leeds General Infirmary (20) to join Tour Two. At the end of Tour Two at the Drayman (34) return to Park Row to see the Frieze (18) and the Black Horse (19).

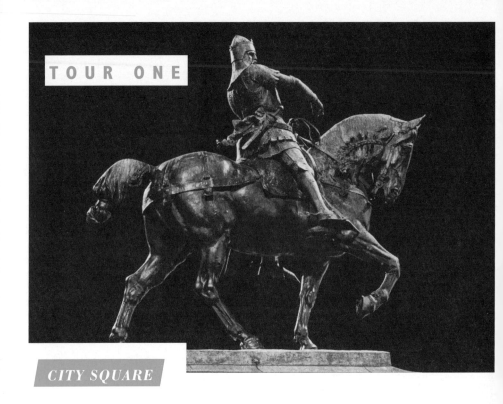

CITY SQUARE

Starts in City Square where you should cross carefully to the central precinct to find the large equestrian statue of the BLACK PRINCE (1). Also here are the FOUR PAIRS OF FIGURE LAMPS (2) and FOUR LEEDS WORTHIES (3-6).

1 EDWARD THE BLACK PRINCE 1903
by Thomas Brock .

Why Edward the Black Prince should mark the city's entrance (by rail) is not immediately apparent. To commemorate Leeds's elevation from town to city in 1893 the city fathers decided to create an open civic space and the future lord mayor, Alderman T Walter Harding, devised and was the major benefactor of a sculptural scheme to decorate it. Major cities display their civic pride, wealth and power through symbols such as sculpture, of which the equestrian statue is one of the most potent. To take its place in the arena Leeds needed a champion. 'The Black Prince' was chosen (somewhat controversially) to symbolise chivalry, good government, patronage of the arts and education, encouragement of industry, and democratic values; the names of men from the Prince's era entwining the pedestal emphasise the allegory. Sir John Chandos (founder-member of the Order of the Garter); Froissart (chronicler of chivalry); Walter de Mannay (soldier); Bertram de Guesclin (military leader); Chaucer (father of English literature); Van Artevelde (encouraged Flemish weavers and dyers to visit northern England, laying the foundations of the textile industry); William of Wykham (Lord Chancellor, Bishop of Winchester, endowed Winchester College, and New College, Oxford, member of the Good Parliament). The bronze low relief panels on the pedestal show land and sea battles, evoking the Prince's heroism against France (particularly topical in the light of contemporary rivalry for Africa's gold coast).

This grand bronze took 7 years to complete and had to be cast in Belgium as it was too large for any British foundry. The Black Prince was brought to City Square in Venetian style by barge from Hull along the Aire and Calder Navigation and unveiled on 16 September 1903. Although the sculptor Thomas (later Sir Thomas) Brock was criticised for 'just a touch of

the stage heroics' the equestrian was an assured success and Brock went on to sculpt the national memorial to Queen Victoria in The Mall, London.

Harding envisaged an equivalent for Leeds of the grand piazzas which graced the centres of the historic Italian city states. For Leeds this would be an equestrian of an heroic royal prince, namesake of the current heir to the throne, set in an illuminated diadem of figure lamps. 4 paladins of Leeds civic pride: Watt, Harrison, Hook and Priestley were added to complete the composition. During the 1960s City Square was rearranged and various elements removed.

2   FOUR PAIRS OF FIGURE LAMPS: MORN AND EVEN 1903 by Alfred Drury .

Originally these lamps encircled the Black Prince on a granite balustrade; now incongruously they stand in line, so loosing the celestial analogy. Drury had recently worked in Paris with the eminent sculptor, Dalou and the lights were inspired by female figures which stand beside lamp standards around the Paris Opera House, representing the Stars of Morning and Night. They demonstrate the turn of the century desire to bring high art to everyday objects combined with an excitement about the new electric street lighting.

Black Prince, Harding affirmed the conservative nature of the Square; Thornycroft would have been the more innovative sculptor, Brock was more heroic. Nevertheless, this remains the most impressive group of late nineteenth century sculpture in Britain outside London and a prelude to The Mall with Brock's Victoria Memorial.

3   JAMES WATT 1903 by Henry Charles Fehr.

City Square commemorates Leeds's elevation from town to city in 1893. Such an event demanded recognition, but the scheme we see today was not the only one to be considered. Suggestions put forward to fill the civic space included a tramway junction, but most favoured a fountain or statue. Erecting equestrian statues then was a popular trend sweeping Europe and America; 'an old clothier riding a packhorse' evoked old Leeds, but (following the example of Richard the Lionheart by Marochetti (1860) outside the Houses of Parliament) national figures Simon de Montford and Henry V were considered and a model by Hamo Thornycroft of Edward I was brought to Leeds. In choosing Brock's

James Watt (1736-1819) was not among the original four Leeds worthies chosen for City Square, but Councillor Wainwright, an engineer, thought that the Scottish inventor's contribution to Leeds's industrial wealth merited his inclusion and made a death-bed offer to donate this bronze statue. Watt's work on the improvement of the steam engine gave the major impulse to the Industrial Revolution and his engines powered many Leeds mills. Watt's inventions were not all industrial, but included a portable machine for drawing from nature in perspective and an apparatus for the construction of sculpture with which he had hoped, 'to produce a reduced copy of Chantrey's bust of myself, fit for a chimney piece, as I do not think myself of importance enough to fill up so much of my friends' houses as the original bust does'. A plaster copy of Chantrey's original is in the Leeds Museum.

4   *JOHN HARRISON 1903 by Henry Charles Fehr.*

When Leeds gained its charter of incorporation from Charles I (1621) Harrison (1576-1657) was the first mayor, deputising for Sir John Savile. This mild-mannered portrayal gives no hint of Harrison's bravery when Charles was held prisoner in Leeds by Parliamentarians: Harrison took the monarch a jug of ale filled with gold coins, an act which led to the confiscation of some of the loyalist's estates by Cromwell. Instead, Fehr emphasises his piety and philanthropy. Harrison provided new premises for the Leeds Free Grammar School, a market cross, almshouses 'for .. indigent persons of good conversation and formerly industrious' and endowed St John's Church, New Briggate (1634), where his oil portrait provided the sculptor with a likeness. The statue was financed by the Planning Committee Chairman, Councillor Boston.

5   *WALTER FARQUHAR HOOK 1903 by Frederick Pomeroy.*

'The great Vicar of Leeds' (1837-59), commemorated all over the city, delivers his sermon to posterity. Acknowledged as the most zealous of Victorian vicars, Hook's 22 years in Leeds resulted in 21 new Anglican churches, 30 schools and 23 parsonages and the rebuilding of the Parish Church of St Peter.

He secured Woodhouse Moor as a public park and served on Royal Commissions for education and the reduction of factory working hours. Hook was still remembered by many in Leeds and *The Yorkshire Post* stressed the need to capture 'the weight and .. impressiveness of "the old Vicar's" massive, leonine head' and his 'dignity, .. character ..(and) rugged power'.

6 *JOSEPH PRIESTLEY 1903 by Alfred Drury.*

Priestley (1733-1804), born locally at Birstall, was a Unitarian minister and scientist. During his Mill Hill Chapel ministry, an adjacent brewery allowed him to experiment with gases emitted during fermentation. He was amongst the discoverers of oxygen, which he called 'dephlogistigated air' and was awarded the Royal Society's Copley Medal for his work on the identification of gases. He published *'A History of Electricity'* (1767), proving carbon conducts a current; Leeds Infirmary used his electrical machine for treating patients with nervous disorders.

Along with *James Watt (3)* he was a member of the famous Lunar Society. With interests in philosophy, politics and religion, Priestley published numerous tracts, but in a volatile age he was seen as supporting the French Revolution and his Birmingham home was burned by a mob (1791), obliging him to emigrate to America.

From City Square walk north past the front of the Post Office building noting four Statues above the doors representing forms of communication by WS FRITH. Turn left along Infirmary Street, crossing East Parade and turning into St Paul's Street opposite. Take the second turning on the right into Park Square in the centre of which stands:

7 *CIRCE 1894 by Alfred Drury.*

Circe, a beautiful but malign young goddess, inhabited the island of Aeaea where she tempts Odysseus's sailors with drugged food and wine making them forget their past before turning them into hogs. Originally Circe held an upturned goblet in one hand and in the other a wand pointing towards the hogs grovelling in the feast at her feet. Also missing is a slash of drapery once grasped by the rearing beast. The tale ended happily, the animals were rescued by Odysseus and turned back into men. Circe was bought by Leeds Art Gallery, the bronze statue received a Medal of Merit when sent to the Brussels International Exhibition (1898) and was specially requested for the Universal Exhibition in Paris (1900).

statue of the young Queen Victoria riding side-saddle and groups of sculpture embellishing the entrance steps. This spirit of civic pride is carved above the door, whilst the guarding lions were an afterthought:

8   FOUR LIONS 1867 by William Day Keyworth Jr.

These popular symbols of British valour were added nine years after the Town Hall's completion in 1858. Inspired by Landseer and Marochetti's beasts guarding Nelson's column they were a roaring success, particularly since Leeds had paid £550 in comparison to London's £11,000. As one councillor exhorted, 'if those in London were worth what they had cost, the public of Leeds had no reason to grumble at the price of these.' Hull-born Keyworth never visited Africa but had observed lions in Regent's Park Zoo.

Continue along Park Square East crossing the Headrow to the TOWN HALL. On the South Frontage you will see the FOUR LIONS (8) and the FRIEZE (9).

TOWN HALL

Leeds has one of the most impressive classical town halls in the country, its broad colonnade crowned by a splendid domed tower. In 1858, architect Cuthbert Broderick had envisaged a piazza in front with a

9

Walk around to the East side entrance of the TOWN HALL where access to the statues inside can be obtained via the doorkeeper. To the left in the front vestibule are statues of the Royal Family (10-12) and to the right in the rear vestibule are statues of local dignitaries (13-14).

9 LEEDS PATRONISING THE ARTS AND ENCOURAGING THE SCIENCES 1858 by John Thomas .

Civic pride is proclaimed above the Town Hall entrance. Leeds (centre) stands before the seat of justice, with owls emblematic of wisdom and supporters of the town arms. To the right are figures of Music (with lyre and pipe), Poetry (Pan, patron of pastoral poets) and Industry (arm on anvil and holding textile samples). To the left, the Fine Arts (with palette, capital and bust - appropriately of Minerva associated with Leeds through her emblem, the owl) and Science (with compass and mathematical globe). In short: commerce, industry, art and science flourish in Leeds.

10 QUEEN VICTORIA 1858 by Matthew Noble.

A visit by the Queen often prompted a statue and when Victoria was to inaugurate the Town Hall (1858) the future Mayor Peter Fairbairn (24) commissioned this work. The gesture was amply rewarded for during the opening ceremony Victoria knighted him. Noble's popularity as a sculptor had already gained him sittings from the Queen (a concession not always granted).

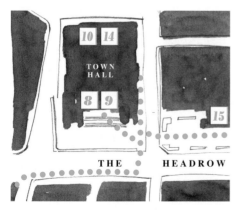

Sculpted from 'appropriately spotless' Carrara marble, she stands in Parliament robes embroidered with the British shamrock, thistle and rose, with 'the pure lily' added as emblematic of her character. Bronze olive and English oak leaves wreathe the base emphasising to contemporaries the work's appearance as 'at once classical and modern'. Originally the statue stood icon-like in the centre of the vestibule (as the choir at the opening ceremony sang) of this 'temple to freedom, to truth and to trade'.

11 PRINCE ALBERT (1865) by Matthew Noble .

ʾrince Albert of Saxe-Coburg-Gotha married his ːousin *Victoria* in 1840. Without any constitutional ːtatus the Prince Consort was nevertheless the Queen's most influential advisor and together they ɪepresented the Victorian ideal of family life. Albert ɔok an active interest in the arts, science and ɪdustry and was among the main instigators of the

Great Exhibition (1851). Within weeks of his death from typhoid fever (1861) suggestions came for a publicly-subscribed memorial as companion to the Queen's statue. The request to move Victoria's statue from the centre of the vestibule to a side apse received Palace confirmation that 'no arrangement would be more gratifying to the Queen'.

12 EDWARD, PRINCE OF WALES AND ALEXANDRA, PRINCESS OF WALES 1872 by Matthew Noble.

Commissioned by Alderman Kitson the busts were also sculpted by Yorkshire-born Noble. Alexandra, Princess of Wales, was regarded as one of the most beautiful women of her day. The busts were approved by the Queen before installation.

13   *EDWARD BAINES 1858 by William Behnes.*

14   *ROBERT HALL 1857 by Dennis Lee.*

Baines came to Leeds as an apprentice printer but, in rags-to-riches style, took over the *Leeds Mercury* making it a leading provincial newspaper and the Whig voice of Yorkshire. Active in local affairs, he helped establish the Mechanics' Institution offering education to working men. In a limited competition for the commemorative statue leading Victorian sculptor, William Behnes, beat Matthew Noble (sculptor of *10-12* and *23*) and Thomas Milnes. Often sculptors never met their subjects and Behnes was amongst the first to use photographs as an aid; this posthumous statue seemed (to contemporaries) 'a somewhat taller and thinner man' than Baines himself, nevertheless 'an example of what a man ought to be'. The newsworthy image was reviewed in *The Times* as 'simple and dignified', and the *Mercury* as 'an admirable work of art'. The statue was first placed in the Victoria Hall where a gallery of local worthies was proposed. This never happened and in 1916 this and its sole companion, Robert Hall, were removed to the Town Hall's rear vestibule.

Hall, the Recorder of Doncaster from 1845-57, wears his robes of office, as if addressing Queen Victoria. He campaigned with Michael Sadler (of Leeds) and Richard Oastler (of Bradford) for the reduction of children's factory working hours. As a Northern Circuit judge he became concerned about juvenile crime and, when elected Conservative MP for Leeds three months before his death, he ardently supported the Reformatories Bill. This 'worthy son of a worthy sire' (the Infirmary has a statue of his father, *Henry Hall (21)*, by Behnes) was active in local Anglican affairs and helped bring the *Rev Walter Hook (5)* to Leeds. Commemorating local men helped unite the town and subscriptions amounting to £600 came from all parties. Civic pride resulted in this commission for a local sculptor, Dennis Lee. This life-size statue is his only surviving major work.

Return to the Headrow, turn left and cross Cookridge Street. On the other side of the Headrow note three statues on the Atheneum building. Walk to the Art Gallery, outside which is the HENRY MOORE:

15 RECLINING WOMAN (ELBOW) 1980 by Henry Moore.

The human figure fascinated Castleford-born Moore (who attended Leeds College of Art) and often, as here, the undulating Yorkshire moorland landscape appears to influence his works. Moore considered that a sculpture should be able to be viewed from all points and that as no two points are alike it would result in an asymmetrical form. For this the reclining figure gave him the greatest compositional freedom and here is one of the last of his monumental works on this theme. The Art Gallery houses other examples of Moore's work including models for this piece and one of his earliest reclining figures.

Enter the Art Gallery (free). In a niche to the left wall is QUEEN ANNE (16). Whilst here you may wish to tour the Art Gallery which has a fine collection of paintings and sculpture and is connected to the Henry Moore Institute where there are changing exhibitions of sculpture.

16 QUEEN ANNE 1712 by Andrew Carpenter.

Royal public statues were less common before Victoria's reign and this, Leeds's earliest civic sculpture, even brought spectators from London. Placed over the entrance to the Moot Hall in Briggate (built 1710, demolished 1828), the original Latin inscription bursts with civic pride: 'Behold! This *LEEDS* statue (distinguished beyond the one at St. Paul's LONDON) of the illustrious *QUEEN ANNE* (allowed by all to be by far the greater representation) Piously consecrated and erected at the sole expense of *WILLIAM MILNER* Esquire Prudent Justice of the Peace, Faithful Subject, Generous Citizen, Opulent Merchant.' The public subscription had failed to raise enough money, so Milner provided the necessary £200 and wanted everyone to know. Sculpted in London and taken from existing images it was based on contemporary portraits of the Queen, here wearing robes of state with the Order of the Garter and holding the gilt orb and sceptre (since lost). The Leeds historian Ralph Thoresby twice visited London to report on progress. Carpenter was a rising sculptor when he received this commission, some years later he was described as 'a Man in his time esteemed for his Skill made many workes for Noblemen & others of distinction ... he was a gross heavy man all wayes.'

The statue was moved to the old Corn Exchange following the Moot Hall's demolition (1828), then to the Town Hall (1868) and finally, the Art Gallery (1887).

Outside the Gallery to the left is the former Garden of Remembrance and the WAR MEMORIAL:

17   *THE LEEDS WAR MEMORIAL 1922 by Henry Charles Fehr.*

Following the First World War many memorials were erected and Lutyens's Cenotaph in London became a popular model. The theme here is a glorious Christian Victory and Peace, personified by bronze figures grouped around the Portland stone cenotaph, originally surmounted by a winged figure of Victory, standing on a globe, holding sword and wreath. To the right St George spears a dragon, alluding to the idea that for many this had been a Christian crusade. To the left 'Invictus Pax' is a hooded female holding a dove, a Christian symbol of hope. The four owls are symbols of Leeds. By 1922 most cities had produced a memorial and Walter Harding, patron of

City Square, returned from Cambridge to move matters along. The memorial was originally erected near City Square where a huge crowd gathered for the dedication ceremony by the leaders of Leeds's religious communities. It was repositioned during the 1930s in the newly-created Garden of Rest. 'Victory' was removed on becoming unstable during a gale in the '60s. Its replacement, by local sculptor Ian Judd, is a figure of Peace laying flowers and was added in 1992.

Cross over the Headrow and turn right into Park Row, heading back to City Square. On the way you will notice on the right three sculptures at No 26 Park Row and opposite on Abtech House an intriguing FRIEZE:

PARK ROW

19 THE LLOYDS BANK BLACK HORSE
1976 by Peter Tysoe.

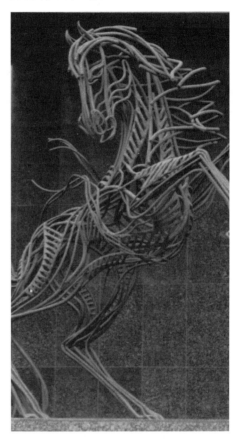

18 FRIEZE, 18 PARK ROW 1902 by
Joseph Thewlis.

The period around the turn of the century was noted for a collaboration between architecture and sculpture to express the function and identity of a building. Here is a particularly good example illustrating Leeds's trading interests and aspirations. Leeds and Carlisle architects, Oliver and Dodgson incorporate the work of a Leeds sculptor to project the commercial identity of the West Riding and Union Bank. The sculpted panel illustrates shipping interests in Africa and investments in railroads in America (countries which Thewlis had undoubtedly not visited). Further symbolic figures divide the panels; Minerva, goddess of spinning and weaving (and so a symbol of Leeds), sits precariously on an Art Nouveau throne, whilst above the entrances boys and girls, supporting the arms of the city, represent purity and plenty (the girls) and peace and justice (the boys).

Further down Park Row there is a recent sculpture of THE BLACK HORSE outside Lloyds Bank:

The bank's familiar emblem is unusually represented here in sculpture. A limited competition, held as the Leeds Branch and Regional Centre neared completion, was won by Tysoe whose powerful image of a rearing horse made from interconnecting solid bars of mild steel suggests the speed and complexity of modern banking.

END OF TOUR ONE

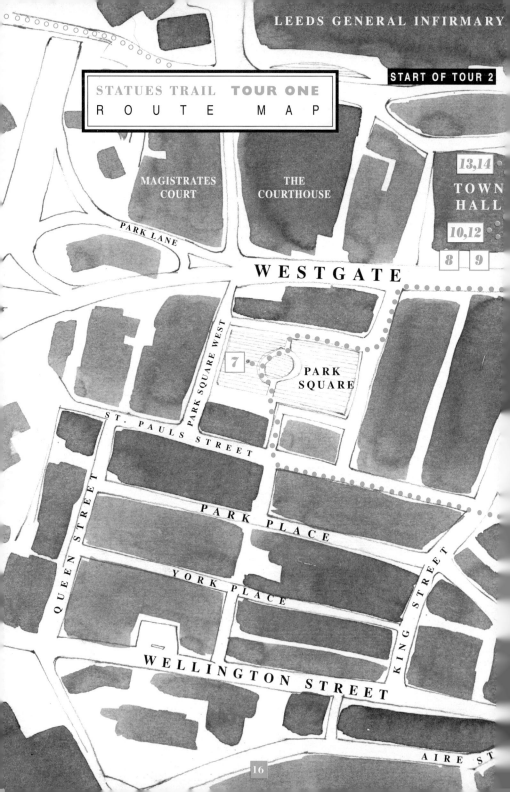

LEEDS GENERAL INFIRMARY

START OF TOUR 2

STATUES TRAIL TOUR ONE
R O U T E   M A P

MAGISTRATES
COURT

THE
COURTHOUSE

13,14

TOWN
HALL

10,12

8 9

PARK LANE

WESTGATE

PARK SQUARE WEST

7

PARK
SQUARE

ST. PAULS STREET

QUEEN STREET

PARK PLACE

KING STREET

YORK PLACE

WELLINGTON STREET

AIRE ST

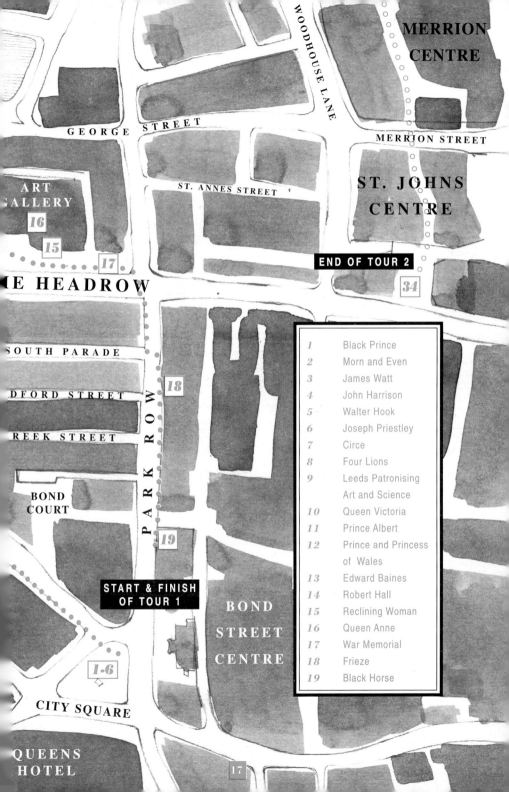

WOODHOUSE LANE

MERRION CENTRE

GEORGE STREET

MERRION STREET

ART GALLERY

16

15

ST. ANNES STREET

ST. JOHNS CENTRE

17

E HEADROW

END OF TOUR 2

34

SOUTH PARADE

DFORD STREET

REEK STREET

BOND COURT

P A R K   R O W

18

19

START & FINISH OF TOUR 1

1-6

CITY SQUARE

BOND STREET CENTRE

QUEENS HOTEL

1	Black Prince
2	Morn and Even
3	James Watt
4	John Harrison
5	Walter Hook
6	Joseph Priestley
7	Circe
8	Four Lions
9	Leeds Patronising Art and Science
10	Queen Victoria
11	Prince Albert
12	Prince and Princess of Wales
13	Edward Baines
14	Robert Hall
15	Reclining Woman
16	Queen Anne
17	War Memorial
18	Frieze
19	Black Horse

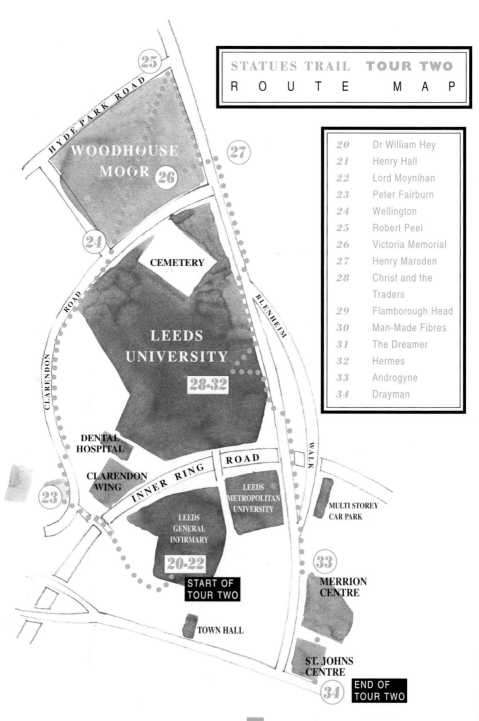

STATUES TRAIL TOUR TWO
R O U T E   M A P

HYDE PARK ROAD

WOODHOUSE MOOR

(25)
(27)
(26)
(24)

CEMETERY

ROAD

BLENHEIM

CLARENDON

LEEDS UNIVERSITY

28-32

20	Dr William Hey
21	Henry Hall
22	Lord Moynihan
23	Peter Fairburn
24	Wellington
25	Robert Peel
26	Victoria Memorial
27	Henry Marsden
28	Christ and the Traders
29	Flamborough Head
30	Man-Made Fibres
31	The Dreamer
32	Hermes
33	Androgyne
34	Drayman

DENTAL HOSPITAL

CLARENDON WING

INNER RING ROAD

WALK

LEEDS METROPOLITAN UNIVERSITY

(23)

LEEDS GENERAL INFIRMARY

MULTI STOREY CAR PARK

20-22

START OF TOUR TWO

(33)

MERRION CENTRE

TOWN HALL

ST. JOHNS CENTRE

(34) END OF TOUR TWO

TOUR TWO

Tour two commences at Leeds General Infirmary, built 1863-8 by architect Sir George Gilbert Scott, following advice from experts including Florence Nightingale. Ask at the entrance hall to see the sculpture.

In the front hall are a series of early twentieth-century bronze wall tablets by *ALLAN G WYON (1882-1962)* commemorating members of the Infirmary: Edmond Trevelyan, Physician to the Infirmary (1914); Walter Thompson, Surgeon to the Infirmary (1926) and Lord Watson, benefactor and member of the Board of the Infirmary (1931).

Go through the entrance hall to the stairway ahead of you. At the foot of the stairs on the left is a statue of DR HEY (20) whilst HENRY HALL (21) is to the right. On the half-landing is a bust of LORD MOYNIHAN (22).

20 *DR WILLIAM HEY 1819 by Sir Francis Legatt Chantrey.*

Hey was the first professional Leeds man to be commemorated by a civic statue. A founder of Leeds Infirmary (1767) (originally on Park Row, but since demolished), Hey was renowned as an excellent surgical operator and introduced improvements in the treatment of hernias, cataracts and dislocations. As Senior Surgeon Hey raised funds through public demonstrations, the most popular gaining over £80, 'the subject dissected being a woman of atrocious character'. Active in civic life, Hey was founding-president of the Leeds Philosophical and Literary Society and was twice Mayor, however his severe denunciations of profanity and vice provoked an

angry reaction, his effigy was burned and he was threatened with violence. *Joseph Priestley (6)* was among his friends, on whose recommendation Hey was made a Fellow of the Royal Society. The statue was commissioned on Hey's death from up-and-coming portrait sculptor, Francis Chantrey (later knighted) and Hey's likeness taken from existing images including a bust by George Bullock (of which the Infirmary owns a plaster). Seated in a fashionable klismos chair Hey relaxes in morning clothes. Broad folds in the coat are contrasted with rippling cravat and wrinkled stockings. Hey was blinded in one eye as a child but Chantrey minimised such scars believing this to be the sculptor's duty.

The commission marks Leeds's aspirations to become the leading cultural centre in the north. A series of exhibitions at the Northern Society for the Encouragement of Fine Art resulted in two particularly fine pieces of public sculpture: John Flaxman's Walker-Beckett monument (1809) in the Parish Church, and Chantrey's Dr Hey.

21   HENRY HALL 1852 by William Behnes.

After 38 years as voluntary treasurer to the Infirmary Hall's colleagues and friends subscribed to this statue by leading portrait sculptor William Behnes, recently engaged to produce Leeds's memorial to *Robert Peel (25)*. Hall began his career in the family stuff business but retired early to devote time to social and political work in Leeds. He was mayor during the 1812 Luddite riots and a founder member and captain of the local Grenadiers.

A prominent Anglican and Tory, with his son *Robert Hall (14)* he helped bring *Rev. Hook (5)* to Leeds Parish Church.

In this companion statue to *Dr. Hey* Behnes shows Hall as if about to rise for action in contrast to Hey's more thoughtful pose. Behnes also produced Hall's bust, now in the Leeds Library.

Despite enormous popularity as a sculptor, William Behnes lacked the financial acumen of his sitter and became bankrupt in 1861. Three years later he was found in a gutter with only threepence in his pocket, and shortly after died in the Middlesex Hospital.

22   LORD MOYNIHAN 1931 by Sir William Reid Dick.

Berkeley Moynihan (1865-1936), created first Baron Moynihan of Leeds in 1929, had a distinguished medical career in Leeds commencing as a brilliant student at the Leeds Medical School and going on to achieve a reputation as the most accomplished surgeon in the country. Having qualified in London he was appointed house surgeon at the Leeds

General Infirmary in 1887. His career in Leeds continued as a consultant and, from 1909, as Professor of Clinical Surgery at Leeds University, he was elected vice-chancellor of that institution in 1924. From 1896 until his death Moynihan was assistant surgeon and then surgeon to Leeds Infirmary. Former patients, students and friends subscribed for this three-quarter length bust by sculptor, Reid Dick. The official unveiling by Hugh Lett, President of the Royal College of Surgeons, was scheduled for 2 October 1939 but postponed owing to the outbreak of war. A ward was also named in his memory. Reid Dick's bust of George V (1933) can be seen in Leeds Civic Hall.

Leaving the Infirmary turn right along Great George Street, take the pedestrian walkway which crosses the inner ring road to the end and arrive in Clarendon Road. On the corner is:

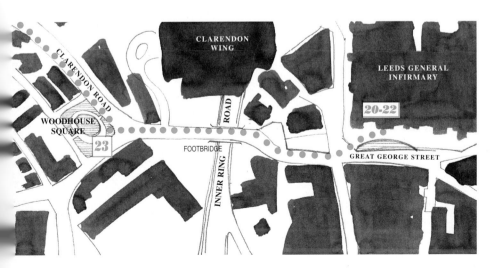

23 *SIR PETER FAIRBAIRN 1868 by Matthew Noble.*

Sir Peter was the epitome of a self-made man, arriving in Leeds in 1824 after an engineering apprenticeship. His improvements to wool and flax-spinning machinery brought huge savings to the textile industry. Backed by a local manufacturer Fairbairn established himself at the Wellington Foundry, New Road End. During the Crimean War he developed engineering tools, expanding to employ about 1,000 men. This was the first outdoor bronze statue of a local worthy and cost £1,000 raised by public subscription. Whilst mayor, Sir Peter was knighted by *Queen Victoria (10)* during the opening of the Town Hall (1858) for which he had commissioned a statue of the Queen. Fairbairn's statue is sited mid-way between his home, Woodsley House, Clarendon Road (where he had entertained the Queen) and the Town Hall.

Continue up Clarendon Road, passing at the top of the hill on the left Fairbairn House, formerly Woodsley House the home of Sir Peter Fairbairn. At the junction with Moorland Road on the corner of Woodhouse Moor stands:

WOODHOUSE MOOR

24 *ARTHUR WELLESLEY, FIRST DUKE OF WELLINGTON 1854 by Baron Carlo Marochetti.*

The hero of Waterloo had been the subject of statues during his lifetime and his death in 1852 prompted more. Despite Wellington's political opposition to the reforms which gave Leeds parliamentary

representation, the town's leaders determined upon a bronze statue for the Iron Duke to stand outside the Town Hall, then under construction. The Sardinian-born Marochetti won the competition, though not without controversy (the sculptor, though Queen Victoria's favourite, was deemed by some too foreign to sculpt a national hero) and £1,500 was raised. The statue was ready three years before the Town Hall's completion so remained boarded up until inauguration (1858). Wellington has remained one of Leeds's most popular statues. The pedestal however was considered disappointing, hardly surprising in comparison to Marochetti's identical figure on top of a high column at Wellington's home, Stratfield Saye.

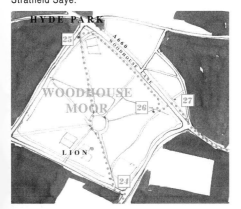

Walk diagonally across Woodhouse Moor to the opposite corner (see map), passing on your left a painted lion fighting a snake (1883) on the grass and at the junction of Hyde Park and Woodhouse Lane find:

25   *SIR ROBERT PEEL 1852 by William Behnes.*

Peel's reputation as statesman and founder of the modern Conservative party rests on his repeal of the Corn Laws (1846); Free Trade measures, benefiting the manufacturing north; parliamentary reform enfranchising Leeds; and the establishment of the police force. The popular Prime Minister's death from a riding accident (1850) caused the first major national demand for commemorative civic monuments. Leeds determined to erect its own. *Edward Baines (13)* voiced civic pride: 'if they were to retain the position ..(as).. the metropolis of the West Riding .. a suitable monument' was needed 'in this great seat of commerce' particularly as Peel 'was eminently the Minister of Commerce'.

A public subscription was raised: lists appeared in banks, the public news room, factories and in Holbeck went from door to door. Anticipating demand for a statue, sculptor William Behnes exhibited a small model and in a limited competition gained the commission. The influential *Art Journal* protested that a politician should be presented in antique style wearing a toga, but was worsted in this argument as the northern woollen magnates insisted on modern dress. Admired for its life-like evocation of Sir Robert addressing the Commons, and for technical innovation, this was the first large-scale bronze to be cast in one piece in Britain; its 2-year progress merited national and local press coverage as well as visits from *Prince Albert (11)*

In August 1852 the statue was placed outside the Old Court House, Park Row (since demolished), the first Peel memorial in the country to be erected.

Walk back along the path parallel to Woodhouse Lane to the corner with Clarendon Road to:

26 *QUEEN VICTORIA MEMORIAL 1905* *by George Frampton.*

Queen Victoria died in 1901 after reigning for 64 years. Memorials were planned throughout Britain and the Empire. Determined that 'loyal Leeds should not lag behind' a statue was proposed to inspire 'a growth of imagination and study' amongst the public and bring about 'the relief of "sordid ugliness" so largely apparent in Leeds'. A limited subscription

raised nearly £8,000. Frampton (later knighted) was much in demand for memorials. Victoria is shown seated on a high pedestal, compensating for her diminutive stature, wearing richly patterned and textured garments and intricate crown daintily perched on top. The figures to the base illustrate contemporary interest in Renaissance art, these sibyls (descended from Michelangelo's Sistine Ceiling), represent British 'Peace' and 'Industry'. The shell-like niches symbolise 'Fruits of the Earth and Sea'. Characteristics of the fashionable 'New Sculpture' are striking contrasts of material, colour and texture, innovative features of Frampton's work.

Unveiled (1905) outside the Town Hall (as in the photograph), it was considered one of the best in the country. The memorial was moved (1930s), along with Peel and Wellington, to make way for a municipal car park itself since removed. It is to be hoped that plans to move it back come to fruition.

Immediately opposite cross Woodhouse Lane to:

27 *HENRY ROWLAND MARSDEN 1878*
by John Throp.

'Johnny on the potted beef', as Leeds cartoonist Phil May called him, commemorates Leeds's most popular Victorian mayor. Born at Holbeck, Marsden's only formal education came from the Sweet Street Methodist Sunday School. After apprenticeship as tool-maker and machinist, Marsden emigrated to America (1848) making his fortune patenting Black's Stone Breaker which he showed at the South Kensington Exhibition in 1862. Returning to Leeds he joined the Council (Liberal) and became Mayor (1873-6) initiating the Leeds Music Festival (1874). Noted for his generosity, he celebrated the Duke and Duchess of Edinburgh's marriage with tea for 1,000 elderly citizens at the Town Hall. The Duke visited Leeds for the opening of the Yorkshire Exhibition of Arts and Manufacture held during Marsden's mayoralty. Over £1,000 was raised for this statue, with contributions from workers at Marsden's Soho Factory. Local sculptor John Throp shows Marsden in mayoral robes, using marble remaining from the Albert Memorial. Pedestal plaques represent Education, Industry and Benevolence; 'The Story of Marsden's Mayoralty ..', 1878 newspapers and a written 'testament' were placed inside.

Continue along Woodhouse Lane towards the city centre and the University. Note the two heads on the Pack Horse Pub, similar to heads on 26 George Street behind the Town Hall. Cross the road to the right hand side and walk on past the University main entrance (the impressive Parkinson Building which has an Art Gallery just inside - and there are several busts in the foyer). Turn to the right through a long portal where the Arts Block and Rupert Beckett lecture theatre is on your left. Inside its foyer is the ERIC GILL (28) facing you down the steps and on the right and left of the corridor in two parts is the AUSTIN WRIGHT (29). This building is open 9-5 Monday to Friday 9-12 noon on Saturdays.

28 CHRIST EXPELLING THE TRADERS FROM THE TEMPLE 1923 by Eric Gill.

This fine relief in Portland stone was commissioned as the University's war memorial by the Vice-Chancellor, Sir Michael Sadler, following a bequest of £1000 from Miss Constance Cross, in memory of her sister, for Sadler to spend as he thought best. Sadler commissioned Gill's rejected design for a London County Council memorial. At that stage both interpreted the parable as a moral endorsement of war in the cause of justice against (German) greed. Sadler envisaged a new liberal Europe suffused with a buoyant Christianity and he believed modern art could best convey such a message. The memorial was to have been made of bronze, but proved too expensive so Sadler suggested the more innovative direct carving method which, together with the work's non-European influences, contrasts with other war memorials reminiscent of an older regime.

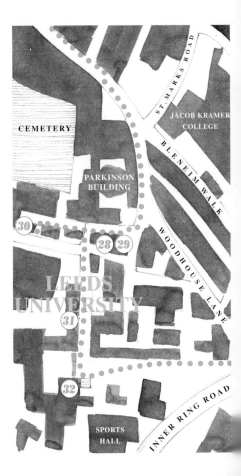

© The University of Leeds

However, unbeknown to the patron, Gill changed the design whilst work was in progress, substituting politically potent contemporary costume for the neutral biblical dress. Having meanwhile become a tertiary novice of the Order of St. Dominic (in celebration of which he added the Dominican hound), the sculptor waged *his* campaign against capitalism in general, exacerbating the growing controversy by declaring to the press, shortly before the dedication ceremony that, 'the money-changers are in modern costume ... because we still have money-changers in England.' Not surprisingly, Leeds businessmen who had helped fund the University and had perhaps lost sons in the war were outraged, but many, including academics J R R Tolkien and Wilfred Childs, were supportive of it as a work of art. Sadler concluded that it was, 'a fine piece of work, but not nearly as good as it might have been'.

29 FLAMBOROUGH HEAD 1962 by Austin Wright.

This work in 2 parts is made from aluminium-coated concrete and was commissioned during Wright's Gregory Fellowship. Its Yorkshire inspiration of cliff and rock formations evidence Wright's belief that nature comes before art, and the organic shapes suggest such origination.

A small diversion towards the Refectory takes you to the Textile Building with its sculpted panel of:

30 MAN-MADE FIBRES 1957 by Mitzi Cunliffe.

American-born Mitzi Cunliffe studied sculpture at Columbia University, then in Paris. Whilst in France she was inspired by Chartres Cathedral and the relationship between architecture and sculpture. Coming to England in 1949 she contributed to the Festival of Britain in 1951, although is perhaps best known for the BAFTA Award (1955), properly called the Jason Trophy (after her son born in that year).

Her interest in Leeds sculpture resulted in the suggestion for the present arrangement of the figure-lamps in City Square, a compromise which helped save them from the scrap heap.

Return and turn right down the steps where you will find the QUENTIN BELL (31) located between levels of the Edward Boyle Library.

31   *THE DREAMER 1983 by Quentin Bell.*

The former Professor of Fine Art provided an elegant solution to the physical requirements of the site, whilst its subject suggests a more meditative aspect of academic life. Constructed of fibre-glass made to look like bronze, the suspension of 'Leeds Levitation' (its alternative title) was made possible by an angled arm constructed in the Mechanical Engineering Department.

Continue down the steps and on the side of the Lecture Theatre block is:

32   *HERMES 1970 by William Chattaway.*

The figure was originally commissioned by the Midland Bank under the title 'Spirit of Free Enterprise'. Saved by the University when the building it ornamented was sold to developers in 1983, it was re-titled 'Hermes' after the Greek messenger to the gods and personification of eloquence and reason, the attributes of a teacher.

The sculptor has endeavoured to retain a truth t material that results here in the emphasis of th craggy roughness of the bronze as it solidifies.

Leave the University via Woodhouse Lan At the crossroads take the subway to th Merrion Centre, passing ANDROGYNE (35 as you mount the steps. Passing through the Merrion Centre on the left can be seen ROWLAND EMMETT'S mobile construction which performs at 11.00am daily. Continuing through the Merrion Centre and St John's Centre brings you to Dortmund Square and the DRAYMAN (34) which ends TOUR TWO. You can pick up TOUR ONE if you are doing the combined walk and so complete Nos 18, and 19 back to CITY SQUARE.

33   *ANDROGYNE 1965 by Glenn Hellman.*

The title of this piece means both male and female, suggesting the work is intentionally perplexing. Simultaneously its appearance is revealed and altered, so it can be seen in various ways. Even the material is ambiguous: fibreglass made to look like concrete. This was the winning entry in a competition held by Town Centre Securities following the opening of the Merrion Centre and chosen by a distinguished panel of judges including the late Sir Herbert Read

(an authority on modern art) and Basil Gillinson (architect of the development). Hellmann, then a student at Hornsea College of Art, shows an awareness of contemporary concerns in sculpture and the strong influence of Moore and Paolozzi.

34   *THE DORTMUND DRAYMAN 1980 by Arthur Schulze-Engels.*

This bronze copy of an original erected by the Altien Brewery in Dortmond (best-known for tales of giants and lager-export) celebrates the tenth anniversary of the civic twinning. It was unveiled by its sculptor in 1980 when Dortmund Square was inaugurated by the civic leaders, Oberburgermeister Samtlebe and Lord Mayor Atkinson.

To pick up TOUR ONE turn right down the Headrow and then left onto Park Row passing Nos. 18, 19 (page 15) before entering City Square.

We hope you have enjoyed this walk round lesser known areas of Leeds as well as seeing a fine range of public sculptures. There are other sculptures mentioned in the appendix which are well worth visiting by car.

A P P E N D I X

OTHER STATUES

Other examples of public sculpture can be found throughout the city, some venues are covered by other 'Walkabouts'. Here are several highlights:

Civic Hall

Bust of George V (1933) by Sir William Reid Dick.

Following the monarch's visit to Leeds Alderman Blackburn, then Lord Mayor, expressed a desire to present a bust. Reid Dick was President of the Royal Society of British Sculptors in 1933 and was noted for his busts and memorial statues.

Bust of Walter Farquhar Hook (1844) by Willam Keyworth.

The bust was presented by Mrs Hook to the Town Hall in 1859. The sculptor's son was responsible for Hook's memorial (see below).

University of Leeds

Statue of Michael Sadler (1837) by Patric Park (Woodhouse Cemetery, St George's Field) removed from the Parish Church. Sadler campaigned with Richard Oastler to introduce the Ten Hour Bill, regulating children's working hours in factories.

Bust of Princess Mary (1909) by FE McWilliam and bust of Frank Parkinson (1951) by Sir William Reid Dick.
Both in the Parkinson Building.

Parish Church of St Peter

Walker-Beckett Memorial (1809-12) by John Flaxman.

A fine Neo-Classical monument to two Leeds men who died at the Battle of Talevera (Spanish Peninsular Wars).

Monument to Thomas Lloyd (1834) by Joseph Gott.

Lloyd was a Leeds wool merchant and leading member of the Leeds Volunteers. The monument is by a local-born sculptor and cousin of industrialist Benjamin Gott, who studied under Flaxman and in Rome.

Monument to William Beckett (d.1863) by Baron Carlo Marochetti.

This is the second work by the flamboyant Sardinian born sculptor in Leeds and commemorates another of the Beckett banking family.

Monument to Walter Farquhar Hook (d.1875) by William Day Keyworth Jr and Anthony Welsh

Hook (see *No.5*) was vicar of Leeds from 1837-59 his Gothic Revival memorial was designed by architect Sir George Gilbert Scott, then completing Leeds Infirmary; the effigy was sculpted by Hull-born Keyworth (see *No.8*) whilst Leeds sculptor, Welsh completed the base.

Also of note is the *Pre-Viking Age Cross* with scenes from the legend of Welland the Smith as well as the Apostles, and the sixteenth-century *Memorial to the Hardwick Family*, a rare survival of its type.

APPENDIX

Church of St John the Baptist, Adel

The south portal has sumptuous Norman carving (though worn) of *Christ in Majesty* at the centre and symbols of the evangelists.

Church of St Bartholemew, Armley

Monument to Benjamin and Henry Gott (1828-31) by Joseph Gott.

The two sons of Leeds industrialist and owner of Bean Ing Mill died whilst on Grand Tour, Benjamin in Athens (1817) and Henry in Paris (1826); the commission went firstly to Flaxman (see above), though when he too died it fell to the Gott's cousin, Joseph to produce a memorial derived from Flaxman's designs. The work was carried out in Rome.

Monument to Benjamin Gott (d1840) by Joseph Gott

Benjamin Gott of Armley House had been a consistent patron of sculptors, helping to promote the statue of Hey by Chantrey in the Infirmary *(20)*.

Church of St Wilfrid, Halton

Statue of St Wilfrid by Eric Gill

Church of St Mary, Whitkirk

Monument to Viscount Irwin (1697) and his wife, by John Nost

The tombchest on which the Viscount reclined has been removed, altering the proportions. Nost's assistant, Andrew Carpenter, helped fit the monument, so introducing to Leeds the sculptor of Queen Anne *(16)*.

Monument to John Smeaton (d1792) by Robert Cooke

Smeaton, the celebrated engineer, designed the Eddystone lighthouse.

Monument to Viscount Irwin (1810) by Joseph Nollekens

This characteristic Neo-Classical memorial is by one of the most prolific and highly regarded sculptors of the period.

FURTHER READING

Beattie S, *The New Sculpture*, New Haven and London 1983

Boorman D, *At the Going Down of the Sun: British First World War Memorials*, York 1988

Kemp B, *English Church Monuments*, London 1980

Leeds Arts Calendar, various including nos *50, 63, 69, 70, 72, 81, 84, 90*

McGuire A and Clark A, *The Leeds Crosses*, Leeds 1986

Penny N, *Church Monuments in Romantic England*, London 1977

Read B, *Victorian Sculpture*, New Haven and New London 1982

Whinney M, *Sculpture in Britain 1530-1830*, Harmondsworth 1964

Whitechapel Art Gallery, 'British Sculpture in the Twentieth Century', 1981 exhibition catalogue

INDEX TO STATUES OF LEEDS